Expl
UnderstandiLaw of Cause
& Effect

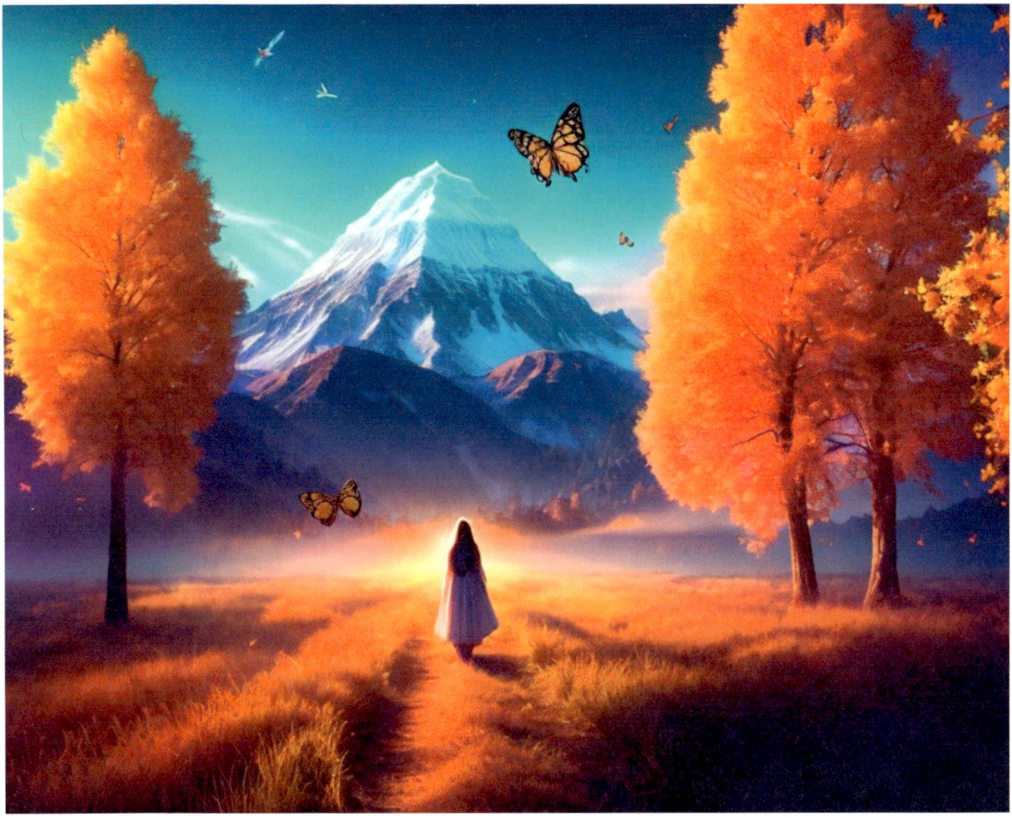

By: James Rondepierre

Table of Contents

Introduction

Forward

Chapter 1: Introduction to Karma
1.1 Defining Karma
1.2 Historical and Cultural Perspectives
1.3 The Significance of Karma in Eastern Philosophy

Chapter 2: The Conceptual Foundations of Karma
2.1 Karma in Hinduism
2.2 Karma in Buddhism
2.3 Karma in Jainism
2.4 Karma in Sikhism

Chapter 3: The Law of Cause and Effect
3.1 Understanding Cause and Effect
3.2 How Karma Relates to Cause and Effect
3.3 The Interplay of Intentions and Actions

Chapter 4: The Three Aspects of Karma
4.1 Sanchita Karma: Accumulated Actions
4.2 Prarabdha Karma: Current Manifestation
4.3 Agami Karma: Future Actions

Chapter 5: Karma and Reincarnation
5.1 Exploring Reincarnation
5.2 The Role of Karma in Rebirth
5.3 Transmigration of the Soul

Chapter 6: The Ethical Dimensions of Karma
6.1 Karma and Morality
6.2 The Law of Dharma
6.3 Living a Dharmic Life

Chapter 7: Understanding Good and Bad Karma

7.1 Positive Karma and its Effects
7.2 Negative Karma and its Consequences
7.3 Balancing Good and Bad Karma

Chapter 8: The Law of Karma in Daily Life
8.1 Karma in Relationships
8.2 Karma in Work and Career
8.3 Karma in Health and Well-being

Chapter 9: Karma and Free Will
9.1 The Influence of Free Will on Karma
9.2 The Limits of Free Will and the Law of Karma
9.3 Balancing Determinism and Personal Choice

Chapter 10: Resolving Karmic Debt
10.1 Understanding Karmic Debt
10.2 Methods for Resolving Karmic Debt
10.3 Forgiveness and Karmic Healing

Chapter 11: Karma and Spirituality
11.1 Karma and Spiritual Growth
11.2 Karma Yoga: The Path of Selfless Action
11.3 Karma and Meditation

Chapter 12: Karma in the Modern World
12.1 Karma in Contemporary Society
12.2 Karma in the Age of Technology
12.3 Karma and Environmental Consciousness

Chapter 13: Karma and Justice
13.1 Karma as Natural Justice
13.2 Karma and Legal Systems
13.3 Examining the Notion of Divine Justice

Chapter 14: Karma and Emotions
14.1 Understanding Emotional Karma
14.2 Karma and Emotional Resilience
14.3 Cultivating Positive Emotional Karma

Chapter 15: Karma and Interconnectedness

15.1 The Interconnected Web of Karma
15.2 Karma and Collective Consciousness
15.3 Compassion and the Alleviation of Suffering

Chapter 16: Karma and Personal Transformation
16.1 Using Karma for Self-Reflection
16.2 Karma and Personal Growth
16.3 Karma and Self-Realization

Chapter 17: Karma and Liberation
17.1 Karma and Moksha
17.2 Breaking Free from the Cycle of Karma
17.3 Liberation and the Dissolution of Karma

Chapter 18: Karma and the Law of Attraction
18.1 Understanding the Law of Attraction
18.2 Karma and Manifestation
18.3 Aligning Karma and the Law of Attraction

Chapter 19: Debunking Common Misconceptions about Karma
19.1 Dispelling Superstitions
19.2 Clarifying Misunderstandings
19.3 Embracing a Balanced Perspective

Chapter 20: Karma and Ethics in a Global Context
20.1 Cultural Variations of Karma
20.2 Applying Ethical Principles to Global Issues
20.3 Promoting Global Harmony through Karma

Chapter 21: Exploring Past Life Karma
21.1 Regression Therapy and Past Life Karma
21.2 Healing Past Life Karma
21.3 Lessons and Growth from Past Life Experiences

Chapter 22: Karma and Family Dynamics
22.1 Ancestral Karma and Family Patterns
22.2 Healing Family Karma
22.3 Karma and the Evolution of Family Relationships

Chapter 23: Karma and Personal Responsibility
23.1 Taking Responsibility for Our Actions

23.2 Accountability and Karmic Consequences
23.3 Navigating Ethical Dilemmas

Chapter 24: Karma and Intentional Living
24.1 Cultivating Intentionality in Actions
24.2 Mindfulness and Karma
24.3 Living a Life of Purpose and Meaning

Chapter 25: The Evolution of Karma
25.1 Karma in a Changing World
25.2 Modern Interpretations and Adaptations
25.3 The Future of Karma

Conclusion

Afterward

About the Author

Certificate of Purchase

Other Books by James Rondepierre

~~~

Introduction

Karma, the universal law of cause and effect, has intrigued and captivated the minds of individuals for centuries. Rooted in ancient Eastern philosophies, karma embodies the belief that every action, intention, and thought we generate carries consequences that shape our present and future experiences. As we embark on this profound exploration of karma, we aim to unravel its intricate web, demystify its complexities, and shed light on its relevance in our modern lives.

In this Redbook, we delve deep into the multifaceted nature of karma, traversing its historical origins, its ethical implications, and its profound influence on personal growth and spiritual awakening. From the ancient teachings of Hinduism, Buddhism, Jainism, and Sikhism to the contemporary interpretations and applications, we aim to provide a comprehensive guide to understanding and harnessing the power of karma.

Forward

Karma, the sacred thread that weaves the tapestry of our lives, guides us on a journey of self-discovery and transformation. In this forward, we invite you to embark on an odyssey of exploration, a pilgrimage into the depths of your own actions and intentions. With each turn of the page, you will encounter ancient wisdom, practical insights, and thought-provoking questions that invite introspection and contemplation.

This Redbook is not merely a compilation of esoteric theories; it is a call to action, a beacon of light that illuminates the path toward conscious living. By understanding karma's profound implications, we hope to empower you to make conscious choices, cultivate compassion, and navigate the intricate dance between free will and destiny.

May this Redbook serve as a companion on your journey, guiding you toward a deeper understanding of yourself, your connections to others, and the world at large. Let us embark together, as fellow seekers, on this transformative expedition into the realm of karma.

Chapter 1: Introduction to Karma

1.1 Defining Karma

Karma, derived from the Sanskrit word meaning "action" or "deed," is a profound and ancient concept that holds immense significance in various spiritual and philosophical traditions. At its core, karma refers to the universal law of cause and effect, positing that every action, intention, and thought generates consequences that shape our present and future experiences.

Karma operates on the premise that our actions have repercussions, much like a ripple effect. It emphasizes the interconnectedness of all beings and suggests that our choices and behaviors carry the potential to impact not only our own lives but also the lives of others and the world at large. Karma teaches us that we are not isolated individuals but rather integral parts of a vast cosmic web, in which our actions reverberate throughout the tapestry of existence.

1.2 Historical and Cultural Perspectives

The concept of karma finds its roots in ancient civilizations and has evolved across different cultures throughout history. It is primarily associated with Eastern philosophies, particularly Hinduism, Buddhism, Jainism, and Sikhism.

In Hinduism, karma is intricately linked to the doctrine of samsara, the cycle of birth, death, and rebirth. It asserts that the quality of our actions in each lifetime determines our future existence, as we carry the consequences of our actions with us from one life to another.

Buddhism views karma as an integral aspect of its teachings on the path to enlightenment. It emphasizes the moral implications of actions and the cultivation of wholesome intentions to break free from the cycle of suffering.

Jainism places a strong emphasis on karma as a factor influencing the transmigration of the soul. It advocates for a life of non-violence and ethical conduct to purify the karmic residues that bind the soul to the cycle of birth and death.

In Sikhism, karma is closely related to the concept of Hukam, the divine order. It teaches that engaging in righteous actions and living in harmony with the divine will
leads to spiritual growth and union with the divine.

1.3 The Significance of Karma in Eastern Philosophy

Eastern philosophy regards karma as a fundamental principle for personal growth, moral responsibility, and spiritual liberation. It provides individuals with a framework to understand the consequences of their actions and the power they hold in shaping their own destinies.

Karma encourages self-reflection and introspection, urging individuals to examine their intentions, motivations, and behaviors. It teaches that cultivating virtuous qualities, such as compassion, honesty, and generosity, leads to positive karmic outcomes, while harmful actions breed negative consequences.

Moreover, karma serves as a moral compass, guiding individuals to make choices that align with ethical principles and contribute to the greater good. It fosters a sense of personal accountability and encourages individuals to take responsibility for the impact of their actions on themselves, others, and the world.

For spiritual seekers, karma acts as a transformative force, propelling them toward self-realization and liberation from the cycle of birth and death. By understanding and transcending the limitations of personal karma, individuals strive to attain higher states of consciousness and unity with the divine.

In the subsequent chapters of this book, we will delve deeper into the intricate workings of karma, exploring its various aspects, ethical dimensions, practical applications, and its role in personal and collective transformation. By embracing the wisdom of karma, we embark on a transformative journey toward greater self-awareness, compassion, and spiritual growth.

Chapter 2: The Conceptual Foundations of Karma

2.1 Karma in Hinduism

In Hinduism, karma holds a central place as a foundational concept. It is deeply interwoven with the belief in samsara, the cycle of birth, death, and rebirth. According to Hindu teachings, every action, intention, and thought leaves an imprint on one's soul, shaping future experiences in subsequent lives.

Hinduism recognizes that karma operates on different levels. Sanchita karma refers to the accumulated actions from past lives, while Prarabdha karma represents the current life's karmic consequences that one must face. Agami karma pertains to future actions and their associated outcomes.

The aim of Hindu philosophy is to purify one's karma through righteous actions (dharma) and spiritual practices, ultimately liberating the soul from the cycle of rebirth. The law of karma in Hinduism provides a framework for understanding the interplay between actions, consequences, and spiritual progression.

2.2 Karma in Buddhism

Buddhism emphasizes the role of karma as a key component in understanding suffering and the path to liberation. The teachings of the Buddha highlight that all actions, intentional or unintentional, carry karmic consequences that shape one's present and future experiences.

Buddhism recognizes that karma is not only created through physical actions but also through thoughts and intentions. It emphasizes the importance of cultivating wholesome intentions, compassion, and mindfulness to break free from the cycle of suffering.

Unlike Hinduism, Buddhism does not hold a belief in a permanent self or soul. Therefore, the focus is on understanding the impermanence and interdependent nature of existence, with karma being an essential aspect of this understanding.

2.3 Karma in Jainism

Jainism places a profound emphasis on karma as a fundamental principle governing the transmigration of the soul. It teaches that all living beings, from the smallest organisms to humans, are bound by the cycle of birth and death due to the accumulation of karmic particles.

Jainism distinguishes between two types of karma: Dravya karma, which is the physical matter that attaches to the soul, and Bhava karma, which influences the mental and emotional aspects of existence. The liberation of the soul from karma is seen as the ultimate goal of Jain spiritual practice.

Jains believe in the power of non-violence, truthfulness, and ethical conduct to purify karma and elevate the soul's consciousness. By practicing asceticism, self-discipline, and right intention, individuals aim to minimize the influx of new karma and gradually eliminate accumulated karmic residues.

2.4 Karma in Sikhism

Sikhism incorporates the concept of karma within its broader teachings on Hukam, the divine order or will. Karma in Sikhism is viewed as the consequence of one's actions and the impact they have on one's life, both in the present and the future.

Sikhism emphasizes the importance of righteous actions, selfless service, and devotion to the divine. Through living in accordance with the divine will, individuals seek to harmonize their actions with the cosmic order, leading to spiritual growth and union with the divine.

Sikh teachings emphasize that karma is not simply a matter of external actions but encompasses one's inner disposition, intentions, and consciousness. The practice of selfless service (Seva) is regarded as a means to transcend personal ego and cultivate positive karma.

In summary, karma is a fundamental concept in Hinduism, Buddhism, Jainism, and Sikhism, each tradition offering unique perspectives and practices. While there may be variations in their interpretations and emphasis on karma, the common thread is the recognition of karma's role in shaping one's destiny, moral responsibility, and the path to spiritual liberation. Understanding the conceptual foundations of karma in these traditions lays the groundwork for a deeper exploration of its applications and implications in the chapters that follow.

Chapter 3: The Law of Cause and Effect

3.1 Understanding Cause and Effect

Cause and effect is a fundamental principle that underlies the workings of the universe. It is the understanding that every action, event, or phenomenon has consequences that follow as a natural result. Cause and effect can be observed in the physical realm, where actions such as pushing a ball result in its movement, or in the realm of emotions, where kind words can uplift someone's spirit.

Understanding cause and effect is essential for comprehending the intricate workings of karma. It is the recognition that every action we take, every intention we hold, and every thought we generate sets in motion a series of effects that shape our experiences and interactions with the world.

3.2 How Karma Relates to Cause and Effect

Karma is intimately connected to the law of cause and effect. It is the mechanism through which cause and effect unfold in the realm of human actions, intentions, and thoughts. Karma teaches us that our actions are not isolated events but part of an interconnected web of causality.

When we engage in positive actions driven by virtuous intentions, we sow the seeds of positive karma, which generate beneficial effects in our lives and in the lives of others. Conversely, negative actions rooted in harmful intentions lead to the creation of negative karma, which manifests as undesirable consequences.

Karma operates on the principle of reciprocity. Just as a seed sown in fertile soil eventually yields a harvest, our actions and intentions create energetic imprints that ripen and bear fruit over time. The effects of karma may not always be immediate or obvious, but they unfold in accordance with the inherent wisdom of the universe.

3.3 The Interplay of Intentions and Actions

Intentions and actions are integral components of the interplay between karma and cause and effect. Intentions serve as the guiding force behind our actions, shaping their nature and karmic implications. They reflect our motivations, desires, and the underlying qualities of our consciousness.

When our intentions are driven by kindness, compassion, and selflessness, our actions align with positive karma. Such actions create a ripple effect of benevolence, fostering harmony, and generating positive outcomes for ourselves and others.

Conversely, intentions rooted in greed, hatred, or selfishness lead to actions that generate negative karma. These actions sow the seeds of disharmony, perpetuating suffering and creating adverse consequences.

It is important to recognize that intentions alone do not determine the entirety of karmic consequences. The actual actions we undertake, the choices we make, and the impact they have on others also shape the outcomes of karma. The interplay between intentions and actions is a dynamic dance, where both elements contribute to the karmic tapestry of our lives.

By cultivating awareness of our intentions and aligning them with virtues such as love, compassion, and mindfulness, we can create a harmonious relationship between our intentions and actions. This alignment allows us to consciously shape the effects we generate, fostering positive karma and contributing to our own growth and the well-being of the world around us.

In the subsequent chapters, we will further explore the multifaceted dimensions of karma, the different aspects of intentions and actions, and their implications for personal growth, ethical responsibility, and spiritual transformation. Through deepening our understanding of the interplay between intentions and actions, we can navigate the path of karma with greater wisdom and create a more harmonious and fulfilling existence.

Chapter 4: The Three Aspects of Karma

4.1 Sanchita Karma: Accumulated Actions

In the intricate tapestry of karma, Sanchita Karma represents the accumulated actions from past lives. It encompasses the sum total of all the actions, intentions, and thoughts we have generated throughout our countless incarnations. Sanchita Karma forms a reservoir of karmic imprints that influence our current and future experiences.

Within the realm of Sanchita Karma, each action leaves an energetic residue, creating a vast storehouse of karmic potential. These imprints shape the patterns and tendencies we carry forward, influencing the circumstances and opportunities that unfold in our lives. Sanchita Karma is akin to a treasure trove, waiting to be tapped into as we traverse our karmic journey.

Understanding Sanchita Karma invites us to reflect upon the continuity of our actions, acknowledging the profound impact they can have across lifetimes. It encourages us to take responsibility for our past actions, recognizing that the choices we make in the present have the power to heal and transform the accumulated karmic imprints we carry.

4.2 Prarabdha Karma: Current Manifestation

Prarabdha Karma refers to the portion of our accumulated karma that manifests in our current life. It is the subset of Sanchita Karma that ripens and becomes the karmic template for our present experiences. Prarabdha Karma represents the predetermined circumstances and events we encounter, providing us with opportunities for growth, learning, and karmic resolution.

Prarabdha Karma is like the script of a play that we are enacting in this lifetime. It encompasses the circumstances of our birth, the genetic and environmental factors that shape our lives, and the specific challenges and blessings we encounter along the way. It serves as a catalyst for our spiritual evolution, presenting us with lessons, tests, and opportunities for karmic healing.

While Prarabdha Karma sets the stage for our current life, it does not dictate our every action or outcome. It provides a framework within which we exercise our free will, making choices that can either perpetuate or transform our karmic trajectory. Prarabdha Karma reminds us that we have the power to consciously respond to our circumstances, navigate challenges, and shape our destiny through mindful choices and actions.

4.3 Agami Karma: Future Actions

Agami Karma refers to the karma we create through our current actions and choices. It represents the karmic potential that will come to fruition in future lives. Unlike Sanchita and Prarabdha Karma, Agami Karma is not predetermined but is influenced by our present actions and intentions.

Agami Karma underscores the significance of our present moment and the power we hold in shaping our future. It reminds us that each action we undertake, each intention we hold, and each thought we generate create ripples of karma that will shape our destiny in subsequent lives. It highlights the importance of cultivating virtuous intentions, practicing mindfulness, and making conscious choices aligned with ethical principles.

Understanding Agami Karma empowers us to live with intention, knowing that our present actions have far-reaching consequences. It encourages us to be mindful of the choices we make, considering their ethical implications and the impact they may have on ourselves, others, and the world at large. By consciously generating positive karma in the present, we lay the foundation for a more harmonious and fulfilling future.

In the subsequent chapters, we will continue to explore the intricacies of karma, further unraveling its profound implications for personal growth, spiritual liberation, and living a life aligned with higher principles. Through a deeper understanding of the three aspects of karma, we gain insight into the interplay between our past, present, and future actions, empowering us to navigate the path of karma with wisdom and intentionality.

Chapter 5: Karma and Reincarnation

5.1 Exploring Reincarnation

Reincarnation, a concept closely intertwined with karma, posits that the soul is eternal and undergoes multiple lifetimes in a continuous cycle of birth, death, and rebirth. This chapter delves into the intriguing phenomenon of reincarnation, inviting us to explore the mysteries of existence beyond a single lifetime.

Reincarnation suggests that our soul carries the imprints of past actions and experiences, shaping our current life and influencing our future incarnations. It offers a framework for understanding the continuity of consciousness and the potential for growth and evolution across multiple lifetimes.

5.2 The Role of Karma in Rebirth

Karma plays a pivotal role in the process of reincarnation. It is believed that the quality of our actions, intentions, and thoughts in each lifetime determines the circumstances, opportunities, and challenges we encounter in subsequent lives. The law of karma provides the mechanism through which the soul navigates the cycle of birth and rebirth.

The experiences and lessons of one life, influenced by the karmic imprints of past lives, serve as catalysts for growth, learning, and spiritual evolution. Positive karma generates favorable conditions, while negative karma may lead to challenging circumstances or obstacles that present opportunities for karmic resolution and growth.

Understanding the role of karma in rebirth encourages us to take responsibility for our actions, recognizing that they have far-reaching implications beyond a single lifetime. It prompts us to strive for self-awareness, ethical conduct, and the cultivation of virtues, as these contribute to the quality of our future incarnations.

5.3 Transmigration of the Soul

The concept of transmigration of the soul accompanies the belief in reincarnation. It suggests that the soul, as it progresses through various lifetimes, may inhabit different forms or bodies, depending on the karmic imprints and evolutionary needs.

Transmigration reflects the understanding that the soul's journey is not limited to human existence but encompasses a vast array of life forms across the cosmic spectrum. It invites us to contemplate the interconnectedness of all beings and the potential for consciousness to manifest in diverse ways.

Recognizing the possibility of transmigration deepens our empathy and compassion toward all living beings. It encourages us to acknowledge the inherent worth and divinity in every form of life, knowing that we are all interconnected in the grand tapestry of existence.

As we continue our exploration of karma, the understanding of reincarnation and the transmigration of the soul expands our horizons, fostering a broader perspective on our place in the universe. It encourages us to embrace the opportunities for growth, cultivate virtues, and navigate the cycle of birth and rebirth with wisdom and grace.

Chapter 6: The Ethical Dimensions of Karma

6.1 Karma and Morality

The concept of karma is deeply intertwined with morality, serving as a guiding principle for ethical conduct. Karma reminds us that our actions have consequences, and it encourages us to consider the moral implications of our choices.

Understanding the relationship between karma and morality requires us to cultivate self-awareness and mindfulness. It invites us to reflect on the intentions behind our actions and the impact they have on ourselves and others. By aligning our actions with ethical principles such as compassion, honesty, and non-violence, we generate positive karma, fostering harmony, and well-being.

Karma and morality go hand in hand, reminding us of our interconnectedness and the responsibility we have towards one another. Through mindful choices and virtuous actions, we contribute to the collective upliftment of society and create a positive ripple effect that extends beyond ourselves.

6.2 The Law of Dharma

Dharma, an integral aspect of karma, refers to the inherent order and righteousness that governs the universe. It embodies the ethical and moral principles that guide our thoughts, actions, and intentions. Understanding and aligning with the law of dharma helps us live a life in harmony with higher principles and cosmic order.

Dharma invites us to discover our unique life purpose and fulfill it with integrity and dedication. By recognizing and honoring our individual talents, passions, and responsibilities, we contribute to the greater tapestry of existence. Living in accordance with dharma brings a sense of fulfillment, meaning, and interconnectedness.

The law of dharma provides a framework for ethical decision-making, helping us navigate the complexities of life with wisdom and discernment. It encourages us to consider the long-term consequences of our actions, promoting a holistic perspective that takes into account the well-being of all beings and the preservation of the natural world.

6.3 Living a Dharmic Life

Living a dharmic life entails integrating the principles of karma and dharma into our daily existence. It involves aligning our thoughts, intentions, and actions with ethical values, fostering personal growth, and contributing to the betterment of society.

A dharmic life emphasizes the cultivation of virtues such as compassion, honesty, humility, and selflessness. It prompts us to practice self-reflection and introspection, nurturing self-awareness and the ability to make conscious choices aligned with higher principles.

Living a dharmic life also involves finding a balance between our individual desires and the greater good. It encourages us to consider the impact of our actions on others and the environment, promoting sustainable and compassionate living. By embracing our interconnectedness, we foster a sense of responsibility and stewardship toward the world we inhabit.

Moreover, a dharmic life is not about perfection but about continuous growth and learning. It invites us to embrace our imperfections and learn from our mistakes, fostering a culture of forgiveness, growth, and personal evolution.

By living in alignment with karma and dharma, we embark on a transformative journey of self-discovery and ethical responsibility. As we strive to embody these principles, we contribute to the creation of a more compassionate, just, and harmonious world.

Chapter 7: Understanding Good and Bad Karma

7.1 Positive Karma and its Effects

Positive karma reflects the accumulation of virtuous actions, intentions, and thoughts. It generates beneficial effects that enhance our well-being and contribute to the overall harmony of existence. By cultivating positive karma, we invite positivity, joy, and abundance into our lives.
Positive karma brings about various effects, both tangible and intangible. It may manifest as favorable circumstances, opportunities, or the presence of supportive and uplifting relationships. It can also lead to a sense of inner peace, contentment, and personal growth.

Additionally, positive karma influences our interactions with others, fostering compassion, understanding, and harmony. It creates a ripple effect, inspiring acts of kindness and generosity that uplift not only ourselves but also those around us. By sowing the seeds of positive karma, we contribute to the creation of a more loving and compassionate world.

7.2 Negative Karma and its Consequences

Negative karma arises from harmful actions, intentions, and thoughts that inflict suffering upon ourselves and others. It generates adverse consequences that disrupt our well-being and perpetuate disharmony in the world. It is important to recognize and understand negative karma to break free from its cycle and foster personal growth.

The consequences of negative karma can manifest in various forms, such as hardships, challenges, or the presence of discordant relationships. Negative karma can also manifest as inner turmoil, guilt, or feelings of discontentment.

Furthermore, negative karma perpetuates suffering and disharmony in the world, contributing to the cycle of pain and conflict. It can create a chain reaction of negative actions and reactions, reinforcing a cycle of negativity.

7.3 Balancing Good and Bad Karma

Balancing good and bad karma involves cultivating awareness, intentionality, and conscious choices. It is a process of self-reflection and transformation aimed at minimizing negative karma and maximizing positive karma.

By recognizing the consequences of our actions, we can take steps to align our intentions and behaviors with ethical values and principles. This involves practicing self-awareness, cultivating empathy, and making choices that promote the well-being of ourselves and others.

Balancing karma also requires acknowledging and learning from the consequences of negative actions. By taking responsibility for our mistakes, making amends, and committing to personal growth, we can break free from negative karmic patterns and create a positive shift in our lives.

Moreover, balancing karma is not solely an individual endeavor. It involves contributing to the greater good, fostering acts of kindness, and promoting positive change in society. By being mindful of our impact on others and the environment, we actively participate in creating a more harmonious and balanced world.

By understanding and striving to balance good and bad karma, we embark on a journey of self-improvement, personal growth, and ethical responsibility. This journey empowers us to create positive change within ourselves and in the world around us, fostering a culture of compassion, harmony, and well-being.

Chapter 8: The Law of Karma in Daily Life

8.1 Karma in Relationships

The law of karma permeates every aspect of our lives, including our relationships. Our interactions with others are governed by the principles of cause and effect, shaping the dynamics and outcomes we experience.

In relationships, karma manifests through the quality of our intentions, actions, and the energy we bring into our connections. Positive and loving intentions generate harmonious relationships, fostering trust, compassion, and mutual growth. On the other hand, negative intentions and harmful actions create disharmony, conflict, and discord.

Understanding karma in relationships invites us to practice mindfulness and cultivate qualities such as empathy, forgiveness, and gratitude. By treating others with kindness, respect, and understanding, we contribute to the creation of positive karma within our interpersonal connections.

8.2 Karma in Work and Career

The law of karma extends to our work and career as well. Our professional lives are influenced by the actions we take, the choices we make, and the intentions we hold.

Karma in work and career highlights the importance of ethical conduct, integrity, and the pursuit of excellence. Engaging in honest and meaningful work, driven by positive intentions, creates a fertile ground for the generation of positive karma.

Conversely, unethical practices, deceit, or pursuing personal gain at the expense of others can generate negative karma and hinder professional growth and success.

By aligning our work with our passions and values, pursuing goals with integrity, and contributing to the well-being of others, we can create a positive karmic impact in our professional lives, fostering fulfillment, and success.

8.3 Karma in Health and Well-being

Karma also influences our health and well-being, highlighting the connection between our actions, intentions, and the state of our physical, mental, and emotional well-being.

Positive karma in the realm of health involves taking care of our bodies, nourishing them with wholesome food, engaging in regular exercise, and practicing self-care. It also includes cultivating positive thoughts, emotions, and maintaining a balanced lifestyle.

Negative karma in relation to health may arise from harmful behaviors, neglecting self-care, or harboring negative emotions and attitudes. Such actions can create imbalances, leading to physical ailments, mental distress, or emotional turmoil.

By recognizing the impact of our choices on our health and well-being, we can cultivate positive karma through conscious and healthy living. Practicing self-love, self-compassion, and making choices that support our well-being contribute to a positive karmic cycle, fostering vitality, and holistic wellness.

Chapter 9: Karma and Free Will

9.1 The Influence of Free Will on Karma

The interplay between karma and free will is a fascinating and complex aspect of human existence. While karma reflects the consequences of our past actions, free will allows us to make conscious choices in the present, shaping the trajectory of our future.

Free will grants us the power to decide our intentions, thoughts, and actions, and it is through these choices that we generate new karma. By exercising our free will with mindfulness, ethical awareness, and compassion, we can align our actions with positive karma, contributing to personal growth, and the well-being of ourselves and others.

9.2 The Limits of Free Will and the Law of Karma

Although free will provides us with choices, it is important to acknowledge the limits of its influence. The law of karma operates within the broader framework of the cosmic order, shaping the circumstances and opportunities we encounter in life.

While we have the freedom to make choices, we are also subject to the consequences of past actions, as well as external factors beyond our control. The law of karma reminds us that we are part of a larger web of interconnectedness, influenced by collective karma and the flow of cosmic energies.

Understanding the interplay between free will and karma allows us to find a balance between personal agency and acceptance of the larger forces at play. It encourages us to make conscious choices while surrendering to the flow of life and trusting in the wisdom of the universe.

9.3 Balancing Determinism and Personal Choice

Balancing determinism and personal choice is a delicate dance that encompasses the realms of karma and free will. While karma sets the stage for our experiences, personal choice and free will provide us with the opportunity to actively participate in our own growth and transformation.

By recognizing the karmic influences in our lives, we gain insight into the patterns and tendencies that shape our experiences. This awareness enables us to make conscious choices, actively working to break free from negative karmic patterns and create a positive shift in our lives.

Moreover, personal choice allows us to respond to life's challenges with resilience, adaptability, and an open heart. It empowers us to make choices rooted in love, compassion, and integrity, fostering personal growth, and contributing to the collective evolution.

By embracing both determinism and personal choice, we navigate the intricate web of karma and free will with grace and wisdom. We cultivate self-awareness, make conscious choices aligned with higher principles, and trust in the unfolding of our karmic journey.

Chapter 10: Resolving Karmic Debt

10.1 Understanding Karmic Debt

Karmic debt refers to the imbalances created by our past actions, intentions, and thoughts. It is the consequence of unhealed karma that manifests as recurring patterns, challenges, or obstacles in our lives. Understanding and resolving karmic debt is a crucial step in our spiritual journey.

Karmic debt presents us with opportunities for growth, learning, and karmic resolution. It invites us to reflect upon the lessons embedded within the challenges we face and make conscious choices to heal and transform.

10.2 Methods for Resolving Karmic Debt

Resolving karmic debt involves conscious effort, self-reflection, and a commitment to personal growth. There are various methods and practices that can assist in this process.

Self-awareness is key in recognizing the karmic patterns and imbalances within ourselves. Through mindfulness and introspection, we can identify the root causes of our karmic debt and the actions needed to bring about healing and resolution.

Forgiveness, both towards ourselves and others, is a powerful tool for karmic healing. By releasing resentment, grudges, and negative emotions, we create space for healing and allow the energy of compassion and forgiveness to flow.

Acts of service, selfless acts, and practicing kindness also contribute to karmic resolution. By engaging in acts of love, generosity, and compassion, we create positive karma that counterbalances negative karmic imprints.

10.3 Forgiveness and Karmic Healing

Forgiveness is a transformative practice that facilitates karmic healing. It involves letting go of past hurts, releasing the emotional burdens we carry, and cultivating compassion for ourselves and others.

Forgiveness is not condoning or forgetting the past but rather liberating ourselves from the grip of negative emotions and resentment. It frees us from the karmic cycles created by holding onto grudges, allowing us to move forward with a lighter heart and a renewed sense of inner peace.

By embracing forgiveness, we contribute to our own karmic healing and create a positive ripple effect in the world. It opens the doors for growth, transformation, and the manifestation of positive karma, fostering harmony, and well-being.

Through understanding, self-reflection, and the practice of forgiveness, we can resolve karmic debt, liberate ourselves from the shackles of the past, and create a future imbued with love, compassion, and harmony. The path of resolving karmic debt is a profound journey of self-discovery and personal evolution, leading us towards greater spiritual awakening and the realization of our true potential.

Chapter 11: Karma and Spirituality

11.1 Karma and Spiritual Growth

Karma plays a significant role in our spiritual growth and evolution. It serves as a powerful catalyst for self-awareness, self-transformation, and the realization of our higher potential.

Understanding the connection between karma and spiritual growth invites us to view life's experiences, both pleasant and challenging, as opportunities for learning and soul expansion. Each encounter, every circumstance, and every relationship we encounter holds lessons that contribute to our spiritual development.

Karma teaches us to take responsibility for our actions, intentions, and thoughts. By cultivating virtues such as love, compassion, and mindfulness, we generate positive karma and create a conducive environment for spiritual growth.

11.2 Karma Yoga: The Path of Selfless Action

Karma Yoga is a spiritual path that emphasizes selfless action as a means to spiritual realization. It involves performing our duties and actions with an attitude of detachment and devotion, without seeking personal gain or recognition.

By practicing Karma Yoga, we transcend the egoic self and align ourselves with the divine will or cosmic order. We recognize that our actions are not driven by personal desires but are offerings to the greater good and the well-being of all beings.

Karma Yoga invites us to engage in actions that benefit others, promote harmony, and contribute to the betterment of society. Through selfless service and acts of kindness, we generate positive karma and deepen our spiritual connection.

11.3 Karma and Meditation

Meditation is a powerful tool for understanding and transcending karma. Through the practice of meditation, we cultivate inner stillness, clarity, and insight, enabling us to observe the workings of our mind, emotions, and intentions.

By developing mindfulness, we gain the ability to observe our thoughts and emotions without attachment or identification. This awareness allows us to make conscious choices, aligning our actions with positive intentions and generating harmonious karma.

Meditation also provides a space for karmic healing and transformation. By cultivating self-compassion and self-forgiveness, we release the burdens of past actions and create space for new patterns and possibilities to emerge.

Incorporating meditation into our spiritual practice allows us to deepen our understanding of karma, transcend its limitations, and experience a profound sense of peace, inner freedom, and spiritual connection.

Chapter 12: Karma in the Modern World

12.1 Karma in Contemporary Society

In the modern world, the concept of karma remains relevant and applicable in various aspects of our lives. It provides a framework for understanding personal responsibility, the consequences of our actions, and the interconnectedness of all beings.

In contemporary society, karma encourages ethical conduct, fostering a culture of integrity, accountability, and compassion. It reminds us that our actions have far-reaching consequences and encourages us to make choices that promote the well-being of ourselves, others, and the planet.

Karma also invites us to cultivate empathy and compassion in a world that often emphasizes individualism and self-interest. By recognizing our interconnectedness, we foster a sense of unity, social harmony, and collective well-being.

12.2 Karma in the Age of Technology

In the age of technology, where our actions can have instant and global impact, karma takes on new dimensions. The choices we make in the digital realm, such as online interactions, social media usage, and information sharing, carry karmic implications.

Karma in the digital age invites us to engage with technology mindfully, considering the ethical implications of our actions and the impact they may have on others. It encourages us to use technology as a tool for positive change, connection, and spreading compassion and wisdom.

Additionally, the digital age provides opportunities for karmic resolution and healing. Online platforms offer spaces for forgiveness, reconciliation, and acts of kindness that can transcend geographical boundaries and foster positive change on a global scale.

12.3 Karma and Environmental Consciousness

Environmental consciousness is closely intertwined with karma. Our actions and choices regarding the environment carry karmic consequences, shaping the well-being of future generations and the health of the planet.

Karma calls us to recognize our role as stewards of the Earth and to make conscious choices that promote sustainability, ecological balance, and the preservation of natural resources. By practicing environmental mindfulness, we generate positive karma and contribute to the healing and restoration of the Earth.

Furthermore, karma reminds us of the interconnectedness of all life forms. It inspires us to cultivate reverence for nature, to acknowledge the intrinsic worth of all beings, and to act in ways that promote the flourishing of the entire web of life.

In the modern world, karma provides a moral compass, guiding our choices and actions in a way that supports personal, social, and environmental well-being. By integrating the principles of karma into our daily lives, we contribute to a more compassionate, just, and sustainable world.

Chapter 13: Karma and Justice

13.1 Karma as Natural Justice

Karma is often referred to as the natural justice that governs the universe. It reflects the understanding that our actions have consequences and that we reap what we sow. Karma operates as a balancing mechanism, ensuring that justice prevails in the cosmic order.

The law of karma reminds us that there is an inherent cause and effect relationship between our actions and the outcomes we experience. It offers the reassurance that justice is not a matter of random chance but is woven into the fabric of existence.

Karma as natural justice encourages us to trust in the wisdom and fairness of the universe. It reminds us that even if justice is not immediately apparent in a particular situation, the law of karma ensures that balance will be restored in due course.

13.2 Karma and Legal Systems

Karma and legal systems exist as distinct but interconnected frameworks for justice. While legal systems aim to provide external justice through human-made laws and regulations, karma operates on a broader, spiritual level, encompassing the consequences of our actions at a cosmic level.

Legal systems establish societal norms and codes of conduct, seeking to ensure fairness, protection, and accountability. They serve as important instruments for upholding justice in human societies, providing a framework for resolving disputes and addressing harm.

Karma, on the other hand, reminds us that justice extends beyond legal systems and societal norms. It encompasses the spiritual and energetic consequences of our actions, intentions, and thoughts. Karma invites us to take personal responsibility for our actions and recognizes that the ultimate justice lies in the balance and resolution of our karmic imprints.

13.3 Examining the Notion of Divine Justice

The notion of divine justice is a complex and multifaceted aspect of karma. It raises questions about the relationship between karma and the divine, and the role of higher forces in the dispensation of justice.

Karma teaches us that we are co-creators of our own destiny and that our actions shape our experiences. It emphasizes personal responsibility and the consequences of our choices, rather than relying solely on external forces to meter out justice.

While the concept of divine justice may vary across different spiritual and religious traditions, karma invites us to explore the idea that the justice prevails and that the consequences of our actions are aligned with our spiritual growth and evolution.

By reflecting on the notion of divine justice, we deepen our understanding of karma and our place in the larger tapestry of existence. It encourages us to seek balance, personal accountability, and a harmonious relationship with the divine, fostering a deeper sense of meaning, purpose, and spiritual connection.

Chapter 14: Karma and Emotions

14.1 Understanding Emotional Karma

Emotions play a vital role in the realm of karma, as they are intricately intertwined with our thoughts, intentions, and actions. Emotional karma refers to the energetic imprints left by our emotional experiences, influencing our present and future experiences.

Understanding emotional karma invites us to explore the ways in which our emotions shape our karmic trajectory. Positive emotions such as love, compassion, and joy generate positive emotional karma, fostering well-being, and harmonious relationships. Negative emotions such as anger, jealousy, and resentment generate negative emotional karma, leading to disharmony and suffering.

By cultivating emotional intelligence and mindfulness, we can navigate our emotional landscape with wisdom and compassion. Awareness of our emotional patterns allows us to make conscious choices, transforming negative emotions into positive ones, and generating harmonious emotional karma.

14.2 Karma and Emotional Resilience

Emotional resilience refers to our capacity to adapt, bounce back, and thrive in the face of life's challenges and emotional upheavals. Karma and emotional resilience are interconnected, as our emotional responses and coping mechanisms shape the karmic consequences we encounter.

Developing emotional resilience involves cultivating self-awareness, empathy, and self-compassion. By recognizing and understanding our emotional triggers and patterns, we can respond to challenges in a way that fosters growth and empowerment, rather than perpetuating negative emotional karma.

Moreover, emotional resilience helps us break free from the cycle of reactive emotions and unconscious behaviors, allowing us to make conscious choices aligned with higher values and intentions. It strengthens our ability to navigate the complexities of life, fostering emotional well-being, and positive karmic outcomes.

14.3 Cultivating Positive Emotional Karma

Cultivating positive emotional karma involves actively nurturing positive emotions and transforming negative emotions into constructive ones. It requires a commitment to self-reflection, mindfulness, and intentional emotional engagement.

Practices such as gratitude, loving-kindness meditation, and forgiveness can contribute to the cultivation of positive emotional karma. By fostering gratitude, we shift our focus to the positive aspects of our lives, generating a positive emotional state. Loving-kindness meditation helps us develop compassion and empathy, promoting harmonious relationships and positive emotional interactions. Forgiveness liberates us from the burden of resentment and negative emotions, fostering emotional healing and creating space for positive emotional karma to flourish.

By consciously choosing to engage with our emotions in a positive and compassionate way, we contribute to our own emotional well-being and generate positive ripple effects in our relationships and the world around us.

Chapter 15: Karma and Interconnectedness

15.1 The Interconnected Web of Karma

Karma reveals the intricate interconnectedness of all beings and the web of cause and effect that binds us together. Every action, intention, and thought creates a ripple effect that reverberates throughout the cosmos, shaping our individual and collective experiences.

Understanding the interconnected web of karma invites us to recognize that our choices and actions not only affect ourselves but also have implications for others and the world as a whole. We are part of an intricate tapestry of interdependence, and our karmic actions have the potential to uplift or harm others.

By cultivating awareness of our interconnectedness, we foster a sense of responsibility and compassion. We become mindful of the impact our choices have on the well-being of others, inspiring us to make choices aligned with love, kindness, and the greater good.

15.2 Karma and Collective Consciousness

Karma extends beyond individual actions and experiences to the realm of collective consciousness. Our collective thoughts, intentions, and actions contribute to the creation of shared karmic imprints that shape the state of the world.

Collective karma reflects the accumulated consequences of societal attitudes, beliefs, and actions. It influences the prevailing social, political, and environmental conditions that we collectively experience. By understanding the role of collective karma, we recognize our collective responsibility for the state of the world and our ability to influence positive change.

Cultivating collective karma involves actively participating in the creation of a more compassionate and just society. It calls for embracing diversity, promoting inclusivity, and working towards the betterment of all beings. By generating positive collective karma through acts of kindness, social justice advocacy, and environmental stewardship, we contribute to the upliftment of humanity as a whole.

15.3 Compassion and the Alleviation of Suffering

Compassion lies at the heart of karma and the alleviation of suffering. Karma teaches us that suffering arises from negative actions, intentions, and thoughts, and that compassion has the power to heal and transform.

By cultivating compassion, we develop a deep sense of empathy and concern for the suffering of others. Compassion motivates us to alleviate suffering and work towards the well-being and happiness of all beings. It serves as a powerful force for generating positive karma, fostering harmony, and promoting social and global transformation.

Compassion encompasses both individual and collective dimensions. Individually, we can practice self-compassion, extending kindness and understanding to ourselves. Collectively, compassion drives us to create a more equitable and compassionate society, where the needs of all beings are acknowledged and met.

Through compassion, we become agents of positive change, actively participating in the healing of ourselves, others, and the world. Compassion is the key that unlocks the transformative potential of karma, leading us towards a more compassionate and interconnected world.

Chapter 16: Karma and Personal Transformation

16.1 Using Karma for Self-Reflection

Karma provides a valuable tool for self-reflection and personal transformation. It invites us to examine our actions, intentions, and thoughts, and to recognize the patterns and tendencies that shape our lives.

By observing our karmic imprints, we gain insight into the areas of our lives that require healing and growth. Self-reflection allows us to identify repetitive patterns, limiting beliefs, and negative behaviors that hinder our personal evolution.

Using karma for self-reflection involves taking responsibility for our actions and embracing the opportunity for growth and transformation. It requires honesty, courage, and a willingness to confront our shadow aspects. Through self-reflection, we can make conscious choices to break free from negative karmic patterns and cultivate positive change.

16.2 Karma and Personal Growth

Personal growth is a fundamental aspect of the karmic journey. Karma provides us with the lessons and experiences necessary for our soul's evolution and expansion.
Embracing karma as a catalyst for personal growth involves seeing challenges and hardships as opportunities for learning and self-improvement. Each karmic encounter offers a chance to develop resilience, compassion, and wisdom.

By actively engaging with our karmic lessons, we cultivate self-awareness, inner strength, and personal transformation. We learn from our mistakes, integrate the wisdom gained, and make conscious choices that align with our higher selves.

Personal growth through karma requires an open mind, a willingness to learn, and a commitment to self-improvement. It is a lifelong journey of self-discovery, self-mastery, and the realization of our fullest potential.

16.3 Karma and Self-Realization

Karma serves as a pathway to self-realization, the ultimate goal of spiritual evolution. Self-realization is the recognition of our true nature and our interconnectedness with the divine and all of creation.

Karma acts as a mirror, reflecting our inner landscape and inviting us to transcend egoic identification. By observing and transforming our karmic imprints, we dissolve the illusions that veil our true selves and come to know the essence of our being.

Self-realization through karma involves surrendering the egoic attachments, desires, and identifications that bind us to the cycle of karma. It is a journey of awakening to our inherent divinity, expanding our consciousness, and experiencing oneness with all that is.

By embracing the transformative power of karma, we embark on a profound journey of self-realization, liberation, and spiritual awakening. Through self-reflection, personal growth, and the cultivation of positive karma, we come to know ourselves as divine beings and embody the truth of our interconnectedness with the universe.

Chapter 17: Karma and Liberation

17.1 Karma and Moksha

Karma and Moksha are deeply interconnected concepts in Eastern philosophy. Moksha refers to liberation from the cycle of birth and death, the ultimate goal of spiritual seekers. Understanding the relationship between karma and Moksha is essential for those on the path of self-realization.

Karma acts as a binding force, keeping individuals entangled in the cycle of birth and rebirth. The accumulation of positive and negative karma determines the nature of future incarnations. However, the dissolution of karma is necessary for liberation or Moksha to be attained.

17.2 Breaking Free from the Cycle of Karma

Breaking free from the cycle of karma involves transcending the limitations imposed by our actions, intentions, and thoughts. It requires self-realization, the recognition of our true nature beyond the realm of karma.

By understanding the workings of karma and taking responsibility for our actions, we can begin to break free from its grasp. Through self-reflection, self-awareness, and the cultivation of positive karma, we gradually dissolve the karmic imprints that bind us.

17.3 Liberation and the Dissolution of Karma

Liberation or Moksha is achieved when all karmic debts are resolved, and the cycle of birth and death comes to an end. It is the realization of our true nature as divine beings beyond the realm of karma.

The dissolution of karma occurs through spiritual practices such as meditation, self-inquiry, and selfless service. By transcending egoic identification and realizing our oneness with the divine, we liberate ourselves from the limitations of karma.

Liberation is not an escape from the world but a state of being in which we are no longer bound by the karmic cycles of suffering and attachment. It is the ultimate goal of spiritual seekers, offering the experience of eternal peace, bliss, and unity with the divine.

Chapter 18: Karma and the Law of Attraction

18.1 Understanding the Law of Attraction

The Law of Attraction states that like attracts like, suggesting that our thoughts, beliefs, and intentions have the power to manifest corresponding experiences in our lives. Understanding the relationship between karma and the Law of Attraction can enhance our ability to consciously shape our reality.

The Law of Attraction operates within the framework of karma. Our thoughts and intentions create energetic vibrations that attract similar vibrations, influencing the karmic patterns that manifest in our lives.

18.2 Karma and Manifestation

Karma influences the manifestation process by shaping the karmic imprints that determine the outcomes we experience. Positive karma generates a vibrational frequency aligned with abundance, joy, and fulfillment, increasing the likelihood of positive manifestations.

Conversely, negative karma can create obstacles, challenges, and undesired outcomes. However, the Law of Attraction provides an opportunity for conscious transformation and the creation of positive karma through intentional thoughts, beliefs, and actions.

18.3 Aligning Karma and the Law of Attraction

Aligning karma and the Law of Attraction involves conscious awareness of our thoughts, intentions, and actions. By cultivating positive karma through ethical conduct, self-reflection, and compassionate actions, we raise our vibrational frequency, enhancing the alignment with positive manifestations.

Practices such as visualization, affirmations, and gratitude can support the alignment of karma and the Law of Attraction. By visualizing and affirming our desired outcomes with positive intentions, we magnetize corresponding experiences into our lives. Expressing gratitude for the abundance already present cultivates a positive mindset and opens the door for further manifestations.

By consciously aligning our karma with the Law of Attraction, we become active participants in the co-creation of our reality. It empowers us to manifest experiences that are in alignment with our higher selves and contribute to our spiritual growth and well-being.

Chapter 19: Debunking Common Misconceptions about Karma

19.1 Dispelling Superstitions

Karma is often associated with various superstitions and misconceptions that can obscure its true essence. Dispelling these superstitions allows for a clearer understanding of karma and its transformative power.

One common superstition is the belief that karma is solely about punishment or retribution. However, karma is not a punitive force but rather a universal law of cause and effect, inviting growth, learning, and self-transformation.

19.2 Clarifying Misunderstandings

Another misconception is that karma operates as a linear and immediate system of rewards and punishments. In reality, the workings of karma are intricate and complex, influenced by multiple factors, including intention, actions, and timing.

Karma is not solely about the external consequences of our actions but also encompasses the internal transformation and growth that occur within us. It invites us to take responsibility for our choices and offers opportunities for spiritual evolution and liberation.

19.3 Embracing a Balanced Perspective

Embracing a balanced perspective on karma allows for a more comprehensive understanding of its nature. Karma is not solely deterministic nor solely reliant on personal choice. It is an interplay of various factors, including past actions, present choices, and the interconnected web of existence.

By embracing a balanced perspective, we acknowledge both the influence of karma on our lives and our capacity to shape our karmic trajectory through conscious choices. It encourages us to take responsibility for our actions, cultivate positive karma, and contribute to the well-being of ourselves and the world around us.

Dispelling superstitions, clarifying misunderstandings, and embracing a balanced perspective empower us to engage with karma in a more informed and meaningful way. It allows us to harness its transformative power and align our lives with higher principles, fostering personal growth, and spiritual evolution.

Chapter 20: Karma and Ethics in a Global Context

20.1 Cultural Variations of Karma

Karma is a concept that transcends cultural boundaries, yet its interpretations and applications can vary across different societies and belief systems. Understanding the cultural variations of karma allows us to appreciate the diverse perspectives and ethical frameworks that shape our global context.

Exploring the cultural variations of karma involves examining how different cultures and traditions understand and apply the principles of cause and effect. It invites us to recognize the richness and complexity of ethical systems worldwide, fostering a deeper understanding and respect for diverse cultural perspectives.

20.2 Applying Ethical Principles to Global Issues

Karma provides a foundation for ethical reflection and action in addressing global challenges. Applying ethical principles derived from karma to global issues such as social inequality, environmental degradation, and human rights violations encourages us to become active agents of positive change.

By recognizing our interconnectedness and the karmic implications of our collective actions, we are called to embrace ethical responsibility and promote justice, compassion, and sustainability on a global scale. This requires us to examine our consumption patterns, advocate for social justice, and actively engage in efforts to protect the environment.

20.3 Promoting Global Harmony through Karma

Karma offers a powerful framework for promoting global harmony and unity. By cultivating positive karma individually and collectively, we contribute to the creation of a more peaceful and harmonious world.

Promoting global harmony through karma involves embracing the principles of non-violence, compassion, and interconnectedness. It calls for empathy and understanding across cultural, religious, and national boundaries, fostering dialogue, cooperation, and mutual respect.

By recognizing the karmic consequences of our actions and intentions, we can actively work towards resolving conflicts, promoting social justice, and creating a world where all beings can thrive. Embracing karma as a guiding principle in our global interactions empowers us to be agents of positive change, building bridges of understanding and compassion in an interconnected world.

Chapter 21: Exploring Past Life Karma

21.1 Regression Therapy and Past Life Karma

Exploring past life karma involves delving into the belief that our current life is influenced by actions, intentions, and experiences from previous incarnations. Regression therapy is one approach that allows individuals to access past life memories and understand the karmic imprints that shape their present circumstances.

Regression therapy provides a valuable tool for exploring past life karma, helping individuals gain insight into recurring patterns, unresolved conflicts, and lessons carried forward from previous lifetimes. Through regression therapy, we can access the wisdom and healing necessary to release karmic burdens and facilitate personal growth.

21.2 Healing Past Life Karma

Healing past life karma involves integrating the lessons and experiences from previous incarnations into our present lives. It requires self-reflection, self-compassion, and a willingness to confront unresolved karmic imprints.

Through various healing modalities, such as energy work, meditation, and inner exploration, we can heal past life karma. This healing process involves forgiveness, releasing negative attachments, and cultivating positive intentions and actions aligned with our soul's growth.

By healing past life karma, we liberate ourselves from repetitive patterns, gain a deeper understanding of our life's purpose, and accelerate our spiritual evolution.

21.3 Lessons and Growth from Past Life Experiences

Past life experiences offer valuable lessons and opportunities for growth. By exploring our past life karma, we can gain insights into our strengths, weaknesses, and soul's journey across lifetimes.

By reflecting on past life experiences, we can identify recurring themes, patterns, and unresolved lessons that may be influencing our present lives. This self-reflection allows us to consciously work on those areas, develop self-awareness, and make choices aligned with our soul's evolution.

Understanding our past life experiences also fosters empathy and compassion for others, recognizing that they too are on their own karmic journey. By embracing the growth and lessons from past life experiences, we deepen our understanding of ourselves and contribute to the collective evolution of consciousness.

Chapter 22: Karma and Family Dynamics

22.1 Ancestral Karma and Family Patterns

Karma extends beyond individual experiences and encompasses ancestral karma and family dynamics. Ancestral karma refers to the accumulated karmic imprints inherited from our ancestors, influencing our family patterns and individual lives.

Exploring ancestral karma allows us to understand the intergenerational patterns and tendencies that shape our family dynamics. By recognizing and healing ancestral karma, we can break free from negative patterns and create a more harmonious and supportive family environment.

22.2 Healing Family Karma

Healing family karma involves acknowledging and transforming the karmic imprints that perpetuate dysfunctional patterns within our families. It requires forgiveness, compassion, and a commitment to breaking free from the limitations of past experiences.

Through conscious communication, emotional healing, and self-reflection, we can create an environment that fosters healing and growth for ourselves and our family members. Healing family karma involves releasing old wounds, promoting understanding, and cultivating love and acceptance within the family unit.

22.3 Karma and the Evolution of Family Relationships

Karma plays a significant role in the evolution of family relationships. It invites us to recognize that our family members are part of our karmic journey, offering opportunities for mutual growth, healing, and soul evolution.

By approaching family relationships with empathy, understanding, and forgiveness, we can transform challenging dynamics and create healthier, more fulfilling connections. Karma reminds us that our interactions within the family unit have far-reaching consequences and offers the potential for deep transformation and love.

By consciously working with karma within the context of family dynamics, we contribute to the evolution of not only ourselves but also our family lineage, creating a positive ripple effect for future generations.

Chapter 23: Karma and Personal Responsibility

23.1 Taking Responsibility for Our Actions

Karma emphasizes the importance of personal responsibility for our actions, intentions, and thoughts. Taking responsibility involves acknowledging the impact of our choices and their consequences on ourselves and others.

By recognizing the power of our actions, we can make conscious choices aligned with positive intentions, ethical principles, and the well-being of all beings. Taking responsibility for our actions empowers us to create positive karmic imprints and contribute to the betterment of ourselves and the world around us.

23.2 Accountability and Karmic Consequences

Accountability is a vital aspect of karma. It reminds us that we are accountable for the consequences of our actions, both positive and negative. Understanding the karmic consequences of our choices encourages us to act with integrity, honesty, and mindfulness.

By accepting accountability for our actions, we foster personal growth, self-reflection, and the opportunity for karmic healing. It allows us to learn from our mistakes, make amends when necessary, and consciously cultivate positive karmic imprints.

23.3 Navigating Ethical Dilemmas

Karma provides guidance in navigating ethical dilemmas by encouraging us to align our choices with higher values and principles. Ethical dilemmas often arise when our actions may have conflicting consequences or when there are no clear-cut answers.

In navigating ethical dilemmas, karma reminds us to consider the long-term effects of our actions, the potential harm or benefit they may cause, and the values and virtues we wish to uphold. By approaching ethical dilemmas with wisdom, compassion, and mindfulness, we can make choices that are in alignment with our higher selves and generate positive karmic outcomes.

Taking responsibility, being accountable, and navigating ethical dilemmas with integrity are essential components of working with karma. By doing so, we actively participate in our own personal growth, contribute to the well-being of others, and create a more harmonious and just world.

Chapter 24: Karma and Intentional Living

24.1 Cultivating Intentionality in Actions

Karma invites us to cultivate intentionality in our actions, recognizing that our intentions shape the karmic imprints we create. By bringing awareness and mindfulness to our choices, we can align our actions with our values, aspirations, and the greater good.

Cultivating intentionality involves reflecting on our motivations and ensuring that our actions are driven by compassion, love, and ethical principles. It requires us to pause, evaluate the potential consequences of our actions, and make choices that generate positive karmic outcomes.

24.2 Mindfulness and Karma

Mindfulness plays a crucial role in working with karma. By cultivating present-moment awareness, we become attuned to our thoughts, emotions, and actions as they arise. This heightened awareness allows us to observe the karmic seeds we are planting and make conscious decisions to nurture positive outcomes.

Practicing mindfulness enables us to break free from unconscious patterns and reactive behaviors. It helps us pause and choose responses that are aligned with our values, fostering positive karmic imprints and personal growth.

24.3 Living a Life of Purpose and Meaning

Karma inspires us to live a life of purpose and meaning, aligning our actions with our soul's calling and contributing to the well-being of ourselves and others. By connecting with our passions, values, and unique gifts, we can lead a purposeful life that generates positive karmic imprints.

Living a life of purpose involves self-reflection, self-discovery, and the pursuit of activities that bring fulfillment and joy. By aligning our actions with our inner values and higher aspirations, we create a sense of meaning and contribute to the collective evolution of consciousness.

Chapter 25: The Evolution of Karma

25.1 Karma in a Changing World

Karma continues to evolve as our world changes. In an increasingly interconnected and globalized society, the consequences of our actions ripple across borders and impact the well-being of diverse communities and the planet.

Recognizing the evolution of karma invites us to explore its implications in contemporary contexts such as technology, social justice, and environmental sustainability. It calls for a broader understanding of the karmic consequences of our choices and the interconnectedness of all beings.

25.2 Modern Interpretations and Adaptations

In response to the changing world, karma has been interpreted and adapted in various ways. Modern interpretations incorporate diverse perspectives, such as psychological, ecological, and social dimensions, offering new insights into the workings of karma.

Modern adaptations of karma emphasize the importance of collective action, social responsibility, and environmental stewardship. They encourage us to address systemic issues and work towards creating a more just, sustainable, and compassionate world.

25.3 The Future of Karma

The future of karma holds the potential for further exploration and understanding. As our consciousness expands, we may uncover deeper insights into the intricacies of karma and its relationship with consciousness, quantum physics, and the nature of reality.

The future of karma also lies in our collective choices and actions. By cultivating awareness, compassion, and ethical responsibility, we can shape a future where karma plays a transformative role in personal and global evolution.

As we embark on this journey of exploring karma, its principles, and applications, we open ourselves to a world of wisdom, growth, and interconnectedness. May our understanding of karma inspire us to live consciously, cultivate positive intentions, and contribute to the co-creation of a more harmonious and compassionate world.

Conclusion

As we come to the end of this Redbook, we reflect on the journey we have undertaken through the intricate tapestry of karma. We have explored its ancient roots, its modern manifestations, and its timeless truths. Throughout this exploration, we have witnessed the profound interconnectedness of all beings, recognizing that our actions have far-reaching consequences that ripple through the fabric of existence.

May the knowledge gained from this Redbook empower you to embrace personal responsibility, cultivate mindfulness, and live a life aligned with higher principles. Let us remember that karma is not a rigid doctrine of reward and punishment but rather a compassionate guide that calls us to awaken to our true potential.

By consciously weaving the threads of our actions, intentions, and thoughts, we shape not only our individual destinies but also the collective destiny of humanity. As we navigate the intricate dance of life, let us embody the wisdom of karma and strive to create a world where compassion, justice, and harmony prevail.

With gratitude for your presence on this transformative journey, we bid you farewell, knowing that the exploration of karma continues with every step you take.

May your path be illuminated by the light of understanding, and may your actions be imbued with the power of love and wisdom.

Namaste.

Afterword: Embracing the Tapestry of Karma with Joy

Congratulations, dear reader, on completing this incredible journey into the depths of karma! As you turn the final page of this book, we invite you to take a moment to bask in the light of inspiration and reflect on the transformative power of understanding and embracing karma in your life.

Throughout our exploration, we have witnessed the profound interconnectedness of all beings, the intricate dance of cause and effect, and the endless possibilities for growth and change. We have discovered that karma is not a daunting web of constraints but a vibrant tapestry that invites us to co-create our reality with joy, love, and intentionality.

As you venture forth from these pages, we encourage you to embrace the wisdom you have gained and apply it to your daily life. Remember that every action, no matter how small, has the potential to make a difference. Your smile, your kind words, and your compassionate deeds can create a ripple effect of positivity that spreads far beyond your immediate surroundings.

Approach each day as a canvas on which you can paint your intentions, aspirations, and dreams. Embrace the power of mindfulness and self-reflection, for they are the tools that enable you to consciously shape the fabric of your karma. Trust in the inherent goodness of the universe, knowing that your positive actions will attract positive outcomes.

As you navigate the complexities of life, remember to be gentle with yourself and others. We all stumble and make mistakes, but it is in those moments that we have the opportunity to learn, grow, and heal. Practice forgiveness, both towards yourself and those around you, for it is through forgiveness that we break free from the chains of past actions and open the door to new beginnings.

Embrace the journey of personal transformation with enthusiasm and curiosity. Explore different paths of spiritual growth, be it through karma yoga, meditation, or acts of selfless service. Cultivate gratitude for every experience, whether joyful or challenging, for each holds a precious lesson that contributes to your evolution.

Finally, let love be the guiding force in all that you do. Love yourself unconditionally, knowing that you are worthy of kindness, compassion, and fulfillment. Radiate love out into the world, embracing the interconnectedness of all beings and celebrating the beauty of diversity.

We hope that this book has ignited a spark within you—a spark of awareness, empowerment, and inspiration. Carry this flame forward and let it illuminate your path, as you continue to explore the vast and wondrous realm of karma.

Remember, dear reader, you are a co-creator of your destiny, and with every thought, intention, and action, you have the power to shape a world filled with love, harmony, and joy.

With infinite gratitude for joining us on this journey,

James Rondepierre

About the Author

James Rondepierre is an acclaimed author and spiritual guide whose works have profoundly impacted readers worldwide. With a rich portfolio of books available on Amazon for Kindle, in paperback, and hardcover, Rondepierre continues to push the boundaries of spiritual and metaphysical literature. His books are celebrated for their depth, clarity, and transformative power, and they are soon coming to Audible, expanding their reach to auditory learners and enthusiasts of spoken word.

Rondepierre's writings encompass a wide array of topics, from the intricacies of meditation and mindfulness to the exploration of past lives and future potentials. Each work serves as a testament to his unwavering commitment to guiding individuals on their spiritual journeys, helping them unlock their highest potential and realize their true selves.

In addition to his literary accomplishments, Rondepierre is dedicated to the study and teaching of ancient wisdom and contemporary insights, offering readers a tapestry of knowledge that empowers them to consciously shape their realities. His latest work, Exploring Karma: Understanding the Law of Cause & Effect, invites readers to delve into the profound interconnectedness of actions and their outcomes, providing a comprehensive guide to understanding and harnessing the power of karma in their lives.

Rondepierre's passion for spiritual growth and personal development shines through in every page of his books, making them essential reading for anyone seeking enlightenment, personal growth, and a deeper understanding of the universe.

~~~

Certificate of Purchase

This certifies that

Name: _____

has purchased

Title: *Exploring Karma: Understanding the Law of Cause & Effect*

Author: James Rondepierre

from

Retailer/Bookstore: _____

on

Purchase Date: _____

Thank you for your purchase. We hope this book guides you on a transformative journey toward understanding the profound law of cause and effect, enriching your life with wisdom and insight.

James Rondepierre

Metaphysical-2-Physical Shop

Peace, love, safety, and blessings. Namaste.

List of Published Books by Author James Rondepierre

1. The Nexus of Worlds: With Bonus Content

Embark on a mesmerizing journey through interconnected realms in "The Nexus of Worlds."

This gripping tale unravels the mysteries of parallel universes and invites readers to dive deeper with bonus content for an enriched experience.

2. Mastering Luck: Comprehensive Guide to Lottery and Gaming Strategy

Discover strategies for navigating the intricate world of lottery and gaming with "Mastering Luck." This comprehensive guide reveals secrets behind mastering the elusive force of luck.

3. Exploring the Infinite Realm: Unveiling the Mysteries of Dreams

"Exploring the Infinite Realm" takes readers on an enchanting journey through the profound mysteries of dreams, delving into the limitless possibilities of the dreamworld.

4. Exploring Karma: Understanding the Law of Cause and Effect

Gain insights into the workings of karma with "Exploring Karma." This book offers a transformative journey into the universal law of cause and effect, guiding personal growth and understanding.

5. Harvesting American Ginseng: A Comprehensive Guide

Delve into the world of American Ginseng with "Harvesting American Ginseng." This guide provides practical insights into harvesting and explores the cultural and medicinal significance of this revered plant.

6. The Precision Prognosticator: Navigating the Path to Accurate Future Prediction

Step into the realm of precision predictions with "The Precision Prognosticator." This guide offers valuable insights into foreseeing the future with accuracy and understanding intuitive abilities.

7. Embracing Serenity: Navigating Life's Challenges with Peace, Love, and Happiness

In "Embracing Serenity," readers are invited to navigate life's challenges with grace, peace, and love. This exploration serves as a guide to finding inner peace and happiness.

8. The Subliminal Brilliance Blueprint: Unleashing Your Hidden Superpowers in Higher Dimensions

Uncover the blueprint of subliminal brilliance with "The Subliminal Brilliance Blueprint." This guide explores untapped potential within higher dimensions, offering a roadmap to unlocking hidden superpowers.

9. Veil of the Night: Unveiling the Vampiric Nature of Humanity

"Veil of the Night" invites readers to unravel the mysteries of the night and explore the vampiric nature of humanity. This tale blends the supernatural with the human experience.

10. Transcending Realities: A Holistic Exploration of Consciousness, Shifting Realities, and Self-Realization: Part I

"Transcending Realities: Part I" takes readers on a profound journey through consciousness, shifting realities, and self-realization, offering a multi-faceted perspective on existence.

11. The Quantum Wealth Code: Unleashing Multiversal Prosperity

Unlock the quantum wealth code with "The Quantum Wealth Code." This guide provides insights into prospering across multiple universes and unlocking abundance in various aspects of life.

12. Whispers of the Soul: Love, Sex, and the Sacred Union

Delve into realms of love, sex, and spirituality with "Whispers of the Soul." This exploration offers deep insights into the sacred union of souls, contemplating the deeper dimensions of human connection.

13. The Symphony of Joy: Embracing Life's Grand Design: Includes Bonus Content!

"The Symphony of Joy" invites readers to embrace life's grand design. This edition includes bonus content, adding extra inspiration and joy to the exploration of existence's beauty.

14. Rediscovering The World: A Journey through Anosmia

Embark on a sensory journey with "Rediscovering The World." This exploration provides a unique perspective on the world through anosmia, offering a captivating and introspective experience.

15. Evolving Unity: A Journey to Enrich All Existence, Elevate All Life, and Uplift Humanity

"Evolving Unity" beckons readers on a transformative journey to enrich existence, elevate life, and uplift humanity, serving as a guide for unity and collective growth.

16. 100 of the Greatest Stories Ever Told

Immerse yourself in "100 of the Greatest Stories Ever Told." This collection promises a journey through captivating narratives spanning different genres and eras.

17. Cosmic Wealth: Unleashing the Mystical Forces of Prosperity and Abundance

Unleash cosmic wealth with "Cosmic Wealth." This guide provides a roadmap to attracting prosperity and abundance by tapping into mystical forces.

18. The Modern Day Holy Bible

Explore spirituality in the modern era with "The Modern Day Holy Bible." This perspective on timeless wisdom invites readers to contemplate profound teachings.

19. The Radiance Within: Embracing the Joys, Pleasures, and Purpose of Human Existence

"The Radiance Within" invites readers to embrace the joys, pleasures, and purpose of human existence, encouraging self-discovery and a deeper connection with life.

20. Ethereal Bonds: Love Unveiled

Unveil the ethereal bonds of love with "Ethereal Bonds." This exploration delves into the mysteries and beauty of love, reflecting on the transformative power of human connection.

21. 100 Stories

Immerse yourself in "100 Stories." This collection offers a tapestry of narratives spanning genres and themes for a rich and engaging reading experience.

22. The Symphony of Infinite Wisdom

Dive into the celestial chronicles with "The Symphony of Infinite Wisdom." This book offers profound insights and timeless wisdom for a deeper understanding of life's mysteries.

23. Miracles: Unraveling the Extraordinary Mystery of Divine Intervention

"Miracles" unravels the mystery of divine intervention, inviting readers to contemplate the extraordinary occurrences that defy explanation and glimpse the miraculous in everyday life.

24. Healing Lupus Naturally: A Holistic Approach

Discover holistic approaches to healing lupus with "Healing Lupus Naturally." This guide provides a holistic perspective on health, offering hope and practical strategies for those with autoimmune conditions.

25. Transcending Realities: A Holistic Exploration of Consciousness, Shifting Realities, and Self-Realization: Part II

"Transcending Realities: Part II" continues the exploration of consciousness, shifting realities, and self-realization, promising deeper insights and reflections.

26. Living with Ankylosing Spondylitis: A Journey to Hope and Healing

"Living with Ankylosing Spondylitis" offers a poignant exploration of resilience in chronic illness, inspiring hope and providing a path towards healing.

27. Exploring the Fabric of Reality: Unveiling the Foundations of Existence

"Exploring the Fabric of Reality" takes readers through the fundamental elements of existence, from quantum mechanics to cosmic mysteries, bridging science and philosophy.

28. Awakening the Infinite: A Definitive Guide to Life Across Dimensions

"Awakening the Infinite" explores consciousness and existence, offering a comprehensive guide to navigating the boundless realms of reality and awakening to infinite potential.

29. Manifesting Miracles: Aligning with the Universe to Fulfill Your Dreams

Transform your life with "Manifesting Miracles." This guide harnesses the universe's power to create your desired reality. Explore practical manifestation techniques, align thoughts with dreams, and achieve prosperity, love, and personal growth.

30. Healing Fibromyalgia: Restoring Energy and Living Well

"Healing Fibromyalgia" provides practical strategies for managing fibromyalgia. Learn to reduce pain, boost energy, and improve well-being with expert advice, dietary tips, exercise routines, and stress management techniques.

31. Infinite Echoes: Navigating Parallel Universes and Cosmic Realities

Journey through cosmic realms with "Infinite Echoes." This exploration delves into multiverse theory, quantum entanglement, and parallel universes, unraveling mysteries and questioning existence's fabric.

32. Dreamscapes: A Journey into the Parallel Universe of the Subconscious Mind

"Dreamscapes" invites readers to explore the subconscious mind. Delve into lucid dreams, emotions, and memories, revealing connections between dreaming and waking life through captivating prose and analysis.

33. The Eternal Quest: A Journey to Enlightenment

"The Eternal Quest" explores the human pursuit of enlightenment. Through vivid storytelling, traverse consciousness landscapes and discover profound insights into the nature of existence and spiritual awakening.

34. Enigma Unveiled

"Enigma Unveiled" takes readers on a journey through history and the supernatural. Blending folklore with mystery, explore haunted estates and cursed artifacts, revealing hidden dimensions and enigmas.

35. Buying Time: Unleashing the Natural Timing of Money

"Buying Time" explores aligning financial decisions with natural cycles. Drawing on economics and psychology, this guide offers strategies for mindful spending, investing, and achieving financial freedom.

All Books Available on Amazon for Kindle, and in Paperback and Hardcover Formats - Also Available on Audible and on Other Various Platforms Worldwide

The end.

Made in the USA
Columbia, SC
26 August 2024